# YOUR KNOWLEDGE HAS VALUE

AF149107

- We will publish your bachelor's and master's thesis, essays and papers

- Your own eBook and book - sold worldwide in all relevant shops

- Earn money with each sale

Upload your text at www.GRIN.com
and publish for free

**Bibliographic information published by the German National Library:**

The German National Library lists this publication in the National Bibliography; detailed bibliographic data are available on the Internet at http://dnb.dnb.de .

**Imprint:**

Copyright © 2016 GRIN Verlag, Open Publishing GmbH
Print and binding: Books on Demand GmbH, Norderstedt Germany
ISBN: 9783668275188

**This book at GRIN:**

http://www.grin.com/en/e-book/337519/swot-analysis-and-operation-management-decisions-of-domino-s-pizza

Ishan Syed

# SWOT analysis and operation management decisions of Domino's pizza

GRIN Publishing

**GRIN - Your knowledge has value**

Since its foundation in 1998, GRIN has specialized in publishing academic texts by students, college teachers and other academics as e-book and printed book. The website www.grin.com is an ideal platform for presenting term papers, final papers, scientific essays, dissertations and specialist books.

**Visit us on the internet:**

http://www.grin.com/

http://www.facebook.com/grincom

http://www.twitter.com/grin_com

# University of Bedfordshire

## MBA
## MARCH 2016

## Managing operations & Projects

## Assessment 1.

## DOMINO'S REPORT

## Student Name:

## Ishan Syed

## 18th May 2016

# Executive Summary

This report emphasis the operation management done by the Domino's pizza delivery company on the basis of three Operation Point Service product, design, Quality Management and Supply chain management of the company. Adding on the swot analysis will have the quick view of dominos to improve their markets. Finally, we have find the conclusion and recommendation including theory into practice and references that will help to improve the company outlets, product services and also to increase their revenue in their future aspect.

## Table of Contents

# INTRODUCTION

This report will analyse the critical operation management on the basis of swot analysis of the chosen company Domino's and their operational management decisions which are Service, product design, quality management, Process, capacity design, location, layout design, human resources, job design, Supply-chain management, Inventory management, Scheduling and Maintenance. The report will discuss the three critical operational management decisions of Domino's Pizza which are service, product design, Quality management and Supply-chain management.

Domino's was started in 1960s by two brothers as the fast food business organisation of pizza food industry. Domino's pizza outlet is globally spread in most of the countries. There head office is located in USA in Michigan, whereas their main franchise and their operation are done from UK markets. They are present across the global. As UK is their quality franchise therefore all food products are supplied from the UK and they control the product and other services of domino's pizza to being delivered. It is known for its faster delivering of pizzas due to which customer can get the hot and fresh pizza to eat at their door steps. Domino's is also known for their quality and its taste which make them different from their competitors which are Pizza Hut, Papa Johns, etc.

After analysing the report, conclusion will be drawn, on the basis of which appropriate recommendation will be given. This will help the company in assessing their current operation management decision as explained in this report and evaluate them for their betterment.

# SWOT ANALYSIS

This report will use the SWOT analysis to classify the STRENGTH, WEAKNESS, OP-PORTUNITIES and THREAT to get a quick summary of dominos pizza strategies position.

| Strengths | Weaknesses |
|---|---|
| - Brand Reputation.<br>- Networking globally.<br>- Cost reduction<br>- Package offer.<br>- Quicker delivery supply. | - Difficulty in handling.<br>- lack of dine-in area. |

| Opportunities | Threats |
|---|---|
| - New Restaurant.<br>- Healthy Menus.<br>- Attract children. | - Change in consumer taste.<br>- Strong competitors.<br>- Health issues. |

## STRENGTH

- Brand Reputation: The reputation of the brand is high due to its more advertising and commitment of delivering faster to the door step create responsibility and assurance to the Brand image.

- Networking globally: With 60 global countries and more than 9000 outlet of the company and their franchises it has very excellent networking globally. The customers of the dominos are loyal to their brand so the company has to take further step by launching new varieties of their product in the market to have strong marketing network with their different outlets and franchises.

- Cost reduction: Less price and more variety with different toppings make people to think. Customers from any class can buy and afford the product at reasonable prize.

- Package offer: Domino's keep an eye on their customer by inventing different offers like "Buy one get one free", "Prize slice week and get 50% off pizzas" etc. so that the customer is being attracted to their franchises by different package outlet. They also provide different offers for student. Dominos also promote their scheme like offers for occasion, different scheme coupons.

- Quicker delivery supply: When it is come for the fastest delivery then there is one brand name comes in the people mind that is Domino's pizza. As the service of dominos pizza is very quick, As the company protocol is to deliver the pizza within 30 min so customers don't have to wait for the long time to have their meal and that makes the name of dominos Brand.

## WEAKNESS

- Difficulty in handling: As the franchises outlet of dominos are spread globally on a large scale therefore it become hard to handle the operations and Quality. Due to difficulties in handling, some of their outlets are closed as it can affect the name of the brand.

- Lack of din-in area: As dominos is the faster delivery company it has most of his delivery outlet, but don't have sitting arrangement where their customer want to sit and enjoy with their love ones. Whereas, dominos competitors like pizza hut, papa johns etc. provide sitting outlets for their customers.

## Opportunities

- New restaurant: Dominos can expand their markets by opening new restaurant by opening their bigger outlet where their customer can have sitting arrangement and parties lounge rather then just delivery options.

- Healthy menus: they can add dietary product in their menu list which are of low calories and low fat, which can make their brand increased in their revenues.

- Attract children: As small children like more fast food, they can offer special meal option with Disney or marvel goodies and toys to attract the children as their competitor does all the time. This can help them to get more loyal customer.

## Threat

- Change in consumer taste: dominos have to always be in touch with their customer about their taste by getting feedback.

- Strong competitor: in the fast growing market dominos can face more strong competitor in fast-food field like pizza hut, papa john's, McDonalds, KFC and more.

- Heath issues: Now-a-days people are more concern about their heath. So it can also decline dominos brand image to fall as Pizza is unhealthy in mature market.

## OPERATIONS MANAGEMENT (OM) DECISIONS

### SERVICE, PRODUCT DESIGN

Service come to fast delivery in pizza, Dominos pizza stands at first place. In menu list they provide variety of supplementary items chicken wing, potato wedges, chicken strippers etc. are offered to the customers as a core product with pizza (Horovitz, 2009). The smooth running of the operations at Dominos help them to provide their customers with tailored pizzas and also offer them with additional wide range of products. To have a look at the product design, dominos is finding it very difficult to cope up with delivering the pizzas to the customers on time in Karachi. Flexibility is combined here to meet the requirements of the customers. The product and service at dominos is considered to be the same as they are delivered on a specified time frame. At dominos, the most two important factor they consider are the convenience and the cost when it comes to the product and service design. To know how Domino's, achieve their success and performance in the market, the product life cycle can be explained briefly.

## Product life cycle

Domino's begin his journey in 1960s as a pizza company and then they slowly moved to United Kingdom (UK) and then to different countries. The concept behind the progress of dominos was the online delivery to the door step emerged and replaced all other traditional procedures. The production in 2009, dropped the sales of the dominos due to taste of the customers was changed. Therefore, dominos pizza implement changes in their menus up to 75% and introduced Choco lava cakes, sandwiches etc. The decline of their customer taste made them realized to change their product according to the consumer taste.

## Re-designing

Domino's re-design their product and openly admitted "Now it's time to change the taste as our customers don't like it any more" said by Russell Weiner. Open feedback of consumer exposed that they don't like the taste and the food quality was not good, openly confessed by Domino's (Charlene, 2011). They use the feedback from the customers as a strategy and re-design their core product by adding more alternative. Dominos re-design their product by involving customers so they can satisfy the customer taste. The re-design process made them to stand again in the competition with their competitor Pizza hut, Papa jones etc. (Hoover, 2013). In figure 1 shows the New Product Development plan of Domino's company.

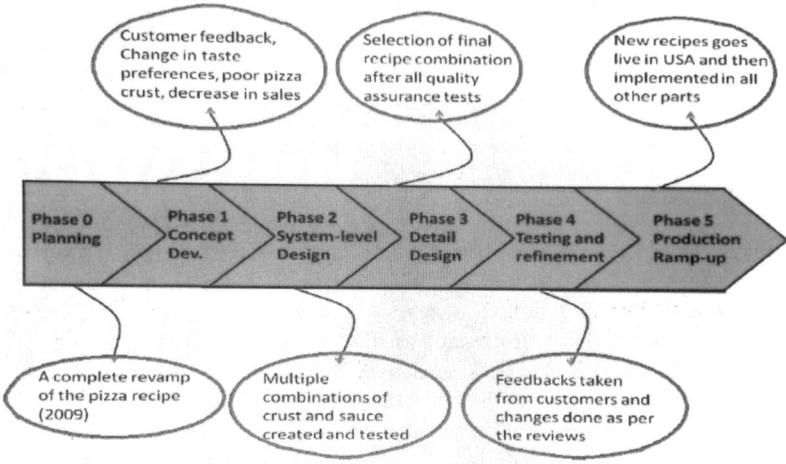

Figure 1. New Product Development (NDP)

## Quality Management

Mahadevan (2010) defines "Total quality Management (TQM) can develop the system in a wide range of organisation by tools, skills, techniques and mind-set which is required to built a quality system that is required to emerged market needs requirement". Domino's always maintained their brand image and the product quality with their customers, described by Ahargrave (2003). Although Dominos' sale is declined heavily due to the video published on the internet about the unethical things done by the workers and also considering it as a unhygienic food.

## Quality Control and Assurance

According to Joseph (2013) it can be seen that there was a growth in their revenue by 6% in UK, when their quality standard was increased. Dominos has the food technologies who ensures the safety of the food product. All the quality related aspects like legality and consistency is maintained for the dominos by them. Dominos also runs a program on food audit for maintaining the safety of products and packaging. All the food samples are well checked and analysed for assuring the food quality with consideration of costumer's feedback for maintaining quality assurance. These settlements are done by Dominos with their suppliers.

Dominos has made a contract with their suppliers including the details of ingredients and specifications required for the quality of the product. In order to maintain the quality of the food, Dominos has a supplier approval procedure where they have an agreement with the suppliers when it comes to the ingredients and packaging of the products. The food being prepared at the dominos are being assessed and audited by the food technologist and also the global standard for food safety.

## Supply chain management

The supply chain model of Domino's primarily consists of Make-to-stock approach. The inventory management and Just-in-Time are factors that not only supports Domino's lean production but also allows efficient functioning. In the environment where prices are constantly fluctuating, Domino's maintains its purchasing power using methods that effectively centralize sourcing.

Dominos company had accepted Make-to-stock as their Supply chain management. Dominos controls and works in on-stock control and Supply chain management based on their lean production. All the dominos franchise globally manages their purchases with the help of their inventory supply chain model. Dominos has a huge capacity of buying the product from the market when the prize goes cheap, this improves the negotiation power with dealers. For example, the Coca-Cola dealers are seen as a partner of the dominos joined their product with them as a supply chain to sell only their beverage drink Coca-Cola to all dominos outlet globally. In figure 2 shows how the supply chain management works.

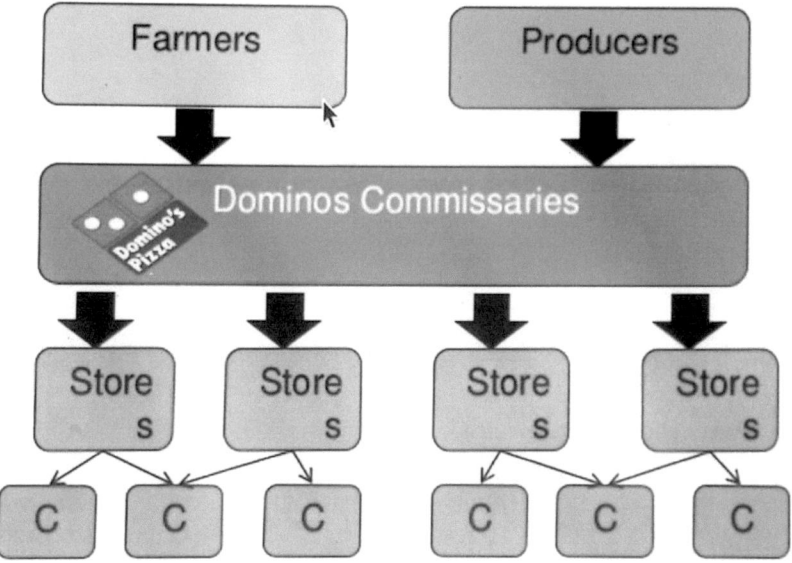

Figure 2. supply chain management model.

## Conclusion and recommendation

This report is based on Domino's pizza delivery service. Domino's is known to be fastest pizza delivery industry but in future can face many problems in busy market as the competition is going tough. By including their 30 min delivery option the can add special week option to attract more customers.

As dominos is the successful organisation in their field of pizza deliveries they can improve their services better in many ways like opening restaurant with large space and dine-in option along with their delivery outlet, they can add heath conscious food product in their menu, and many more things as their competitor does to stand first in the segment of fast growing market. They should also have focused on the children activities and special food item including Disney and marvel toys and goodies to attract the children this can help them to make double customer like children and their parents both having two meals.

The use of supply chain Management is going in a correct path but the can give priority to the quality management to improve their quality and reducing their wastage. Moreover, they can increase advertisement and social media promotion so they can attract the emotion connection with their pizza lover's consumers.

# References

Abilla, p. (2010), Strategic Supply chain: Domino's Pizza Online, available at:
http://www.shmula.com/strategic-supply-chain-dominos-pizza-online/9243/

Ahargrave, S. (2003), http://www.bized.co.uk/comfact/domino/domin-dex.htm?page=14.

Mahadevan, B. (2010). *Operations Management: Theory and Practice*, Second Edition, Pearson India.

Dominos, (2013), The Dominos Franchise story, available at: http://www.dominos.uk.com/franchising/

Horovitz, B. (2009), Domino's Pizza delivers change in its core pizza recipe:
http://usatoday30.usatoday.com?money/industries/food/2009-12-16-dominos16_ST_N.htm

joseph, S. (2013). Dominos pushes it's 'greatness' in brands add: http://www.marketingweek.co.uk/news/dominos-pushes-its-greatness-in-brand-ads/4007846.article.

Hoovers, A D&B Company. (2013), Top competitors for Pizza hut: http://www.hoovers.com/company-information/cs/competition.Pizza_Hut_Inc.99d2e79dc677be.html.

Charlene, L. (2011) Harvard Business Review: The Art of Admitting Failure,
http://blogs.hbr.org/cs/2011/03/the_art_of_admitting_failure.html.

# YOUR KNOWLEDGE HAS VALUE

- We will publish your bachelor's and
  master's thesis, essays and papers

- Your own eBook and book -
  sold worldwide in all relevant shops

- Earn money with each sale

Upload your text at www.GRIN.com
and publish for free